12 Vols.

EN:2.6-3.1

490 - 620

MW01470348

Our Planet Earth

Publisher: **Bellwether Media / Blastoff! Readers**
Library Binding

Gumdrop Price $222.00 ***Purchase & Save!***
Publisher's List Price $323.40

Animals chatter throughout rain forests. Sand whirls across deserts. Currents course down rivers. Earth is covered in breathtaking landforms that play a special role in making our planet unique. In this series, readers will learn about each landform, including what sets them apart, what plants and animals call them home and how people use them. Special features such as diagrams, landform profiles and more guide readers as they discover each natural wonder!

Additional Series :
BLW1330 English eBook

	Title	Dewey	©	Price
Ar Le Fp	Caves	551.4	22	$18.95
Le Fp	Coral Reefs	577.7	22	$18.95
Ar Le Fp	Deserts	551.4	22	$18.95
Le Fp	Forests	634.9	22	$18.95
Le Fp	Glaciers	551.3	22	$18.95
Le Fp	Lakes	577.6	22	$18.95
Le Fp	Mountains	551.4	22	$18.95
Ar Le Fp	Oceans	551.4	22	$18.95
Ar Le Fp	Prairies	577.4	22	$18.95
Ar Le Fp	Rain Forests	577.3	22	$18.95
Ar Le Fp	Rivers	551.4	22	$18.95
Le Fp	Wetlands	333.9	22	$18.95

GD FIELD : 8/15/2023 (6x8½) **USD**

Titles may be purchased individually.

more

10 Vols.

EN:2.4-2.9

480 - 620

O - O

BLW1344
Title

How It Works

Publisher: **Bellwether Media / Blastoff! Readers**
Library Binding

Gumdrop Price $185.00 ***Purchase & Save!***
Publisher's List Price $269.50

Submarines dive, rockets soar to space and computers process information. But how do these things work? In this title, readers will explore the science behind common machines and vehicles through leveled text and engaging photographs. Special features show the machine's parts, break down how they work and explain what people do to control the machine. Each book closes by discussing what future machines will look like and asking readers to join in.

Additional Series :
BLW1351 English eBook

	Title	Dewey	©	Price
Le	Airplanes	629.1	22	$18.95
Le	Cars	629.2	22	$18.95
Le	Cell Phones	621.3	22	$18.95
Le	Computers	004	22	$18.95
Ar Le Fp	Electric Guitars	787.8	23	$18.95
Ar Le Fp	Helicopters	387.7	23	$18.95
Le	Rockets	621.4	22	$18.95
Ar Le Fp	Roller Coasters	791.0	23	$18.95
Le	Submarines	623.8	22	$18.95
Ar Le Fp	Trains	625.1	23	$18.95

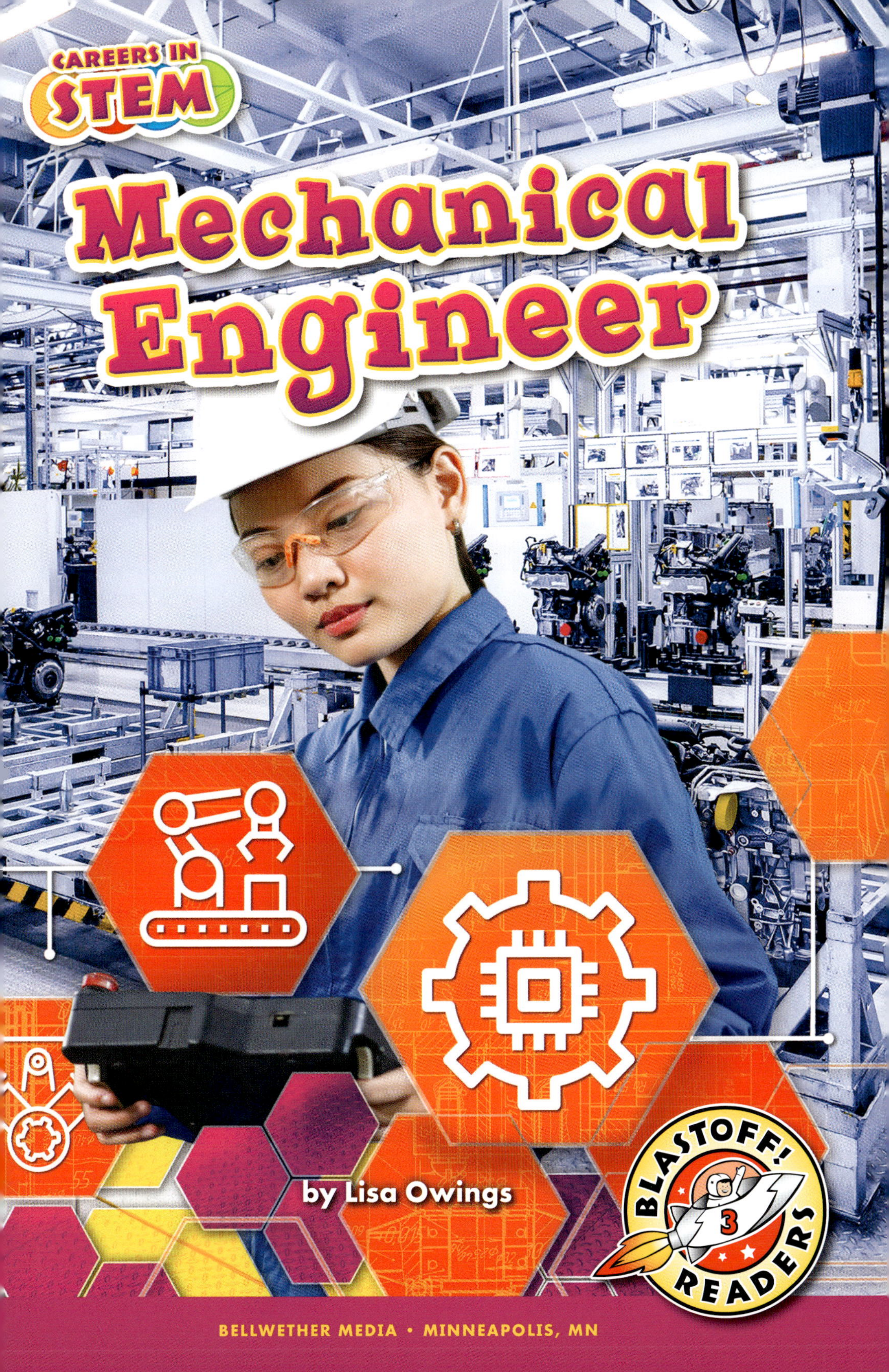
CAREERS IN STEM
Mechanical Engineer
by Lisa Owings
BLASTOFF! READERS
3
BELLWETHER MEDIA • MINNEAPOLIS, MN

Blastoff! Readers are carefully developed by literacy experts to build reading stamina and move students toward fluency by combining standards-based content with developmentally appropriate text.

Level 1 provides the most support through repetition of high-frequency words, light text, predictable sentence patterns, and strong visual support.

Level 2 offers early readers a bit more challenge through varied sentences, increased text load, and text-supportive special features.

Level 3 advances early-fluent readers toward fluency through increased text load, less reliance on photos, advancing concepts, longer sentences, and more complex special features.

★ **Blastoff! Universe**

Reading Level

Grade K

Grades 1–3

Grade 4

This edition first published in 2024 by Bellwether Media, Inc.

Library of Congress Cataloging-in-Publication Data

Names: Owings, Lisa, author.
Title: Mechanical engineer / by Lisa Owings.
Description: Minneapolis, MN : Bellwether Media, 2024. | Series: Blastoff! readers. Careers in STEM | Includes bibliographical references and index. | Audience: Ages 5-8 | Audience: Grades 2-3 | Summary: "Simple text and full-color photography introduce beginning readers to mechanical engineers. Developed by literacy experts for students in kindergarten through third grade"– Provided by publisher.
Identifiers: LCCN 2023001655 (print) | LCCN 2023001656 (ebook) | ISBN 9798886874389 | ISBN 9798886876260 (ebook)
Subjects: LCSH: Mechanical engineering–Juvenile literature.
Classification: LCC TJ147 .O828 2024 (print) | LCC TJ147 (ebook) | DDC 621–dc23/eng/20230118
LC record available at https://lccn.loc.gov/2023001655
LC ebook record available at https://lccn.loc.gov/2023001656

Editor: Betsy Rathburn Designer: Andrea Schneider

Printed in the United States of America, North Mankato, MN.

Table of Contents

Building New Tools

A mechanical engineer works on her computer. She is making a new **prosthetic** hand. Its **sensors** will let users feel and hold objects.

Her **design** will help many people!

prosthetic hand

What Is a Mechanical Engineer?

Mechanical engineers design, test, and build things. They use computers to do their work. They test for safety and **quality**.

Most work in offices. They may also visit work sites or **labs**.

Mechanical Engineering in Real Life

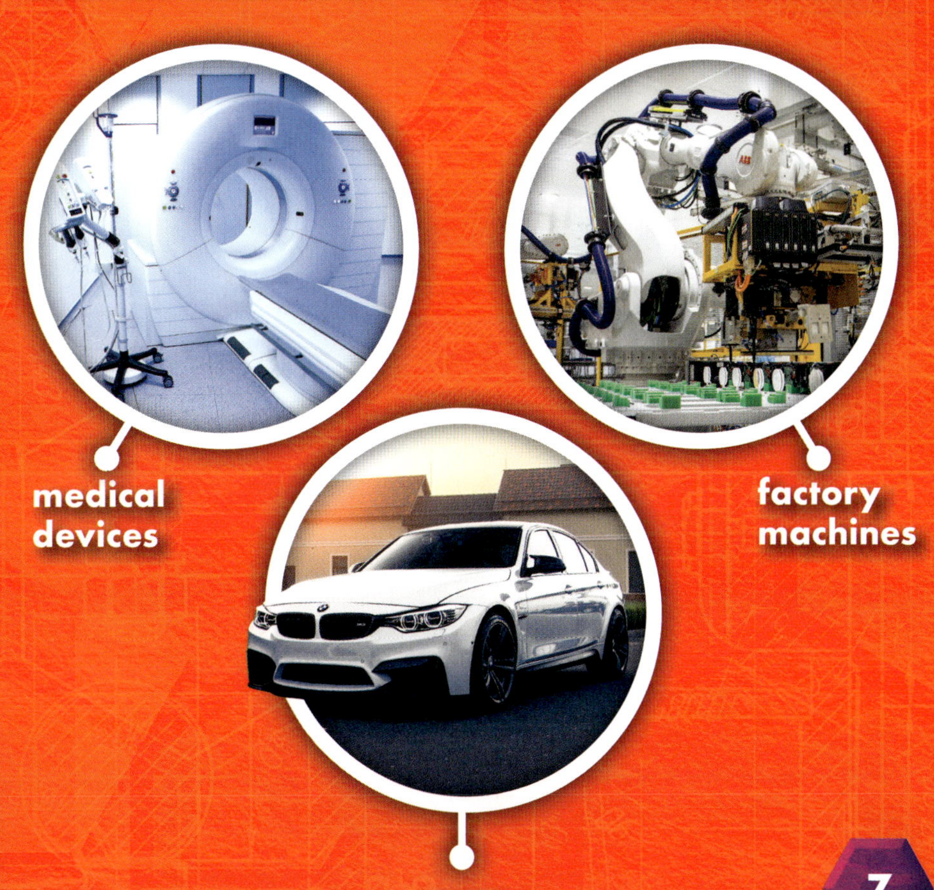

Mechanical engineers make new machines. They also make better parts for old machines.

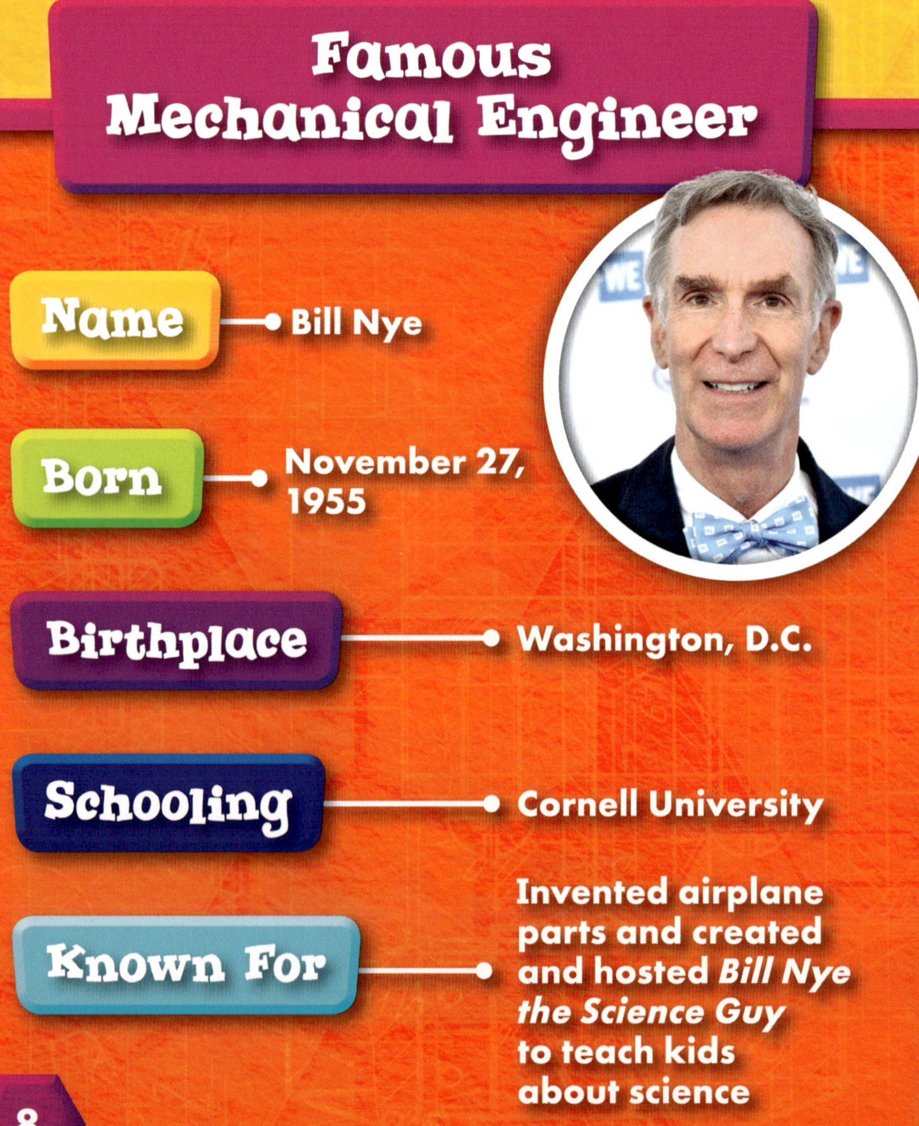

Their work can make the planet healthier. It can make people's lives safer and easier!

Some mechanical engineers work on machines that use fewer **fossil fuels**. They help fight **climate change**.

Others make **medical devices**. These tools help doctors work. They help people live healthier lives!

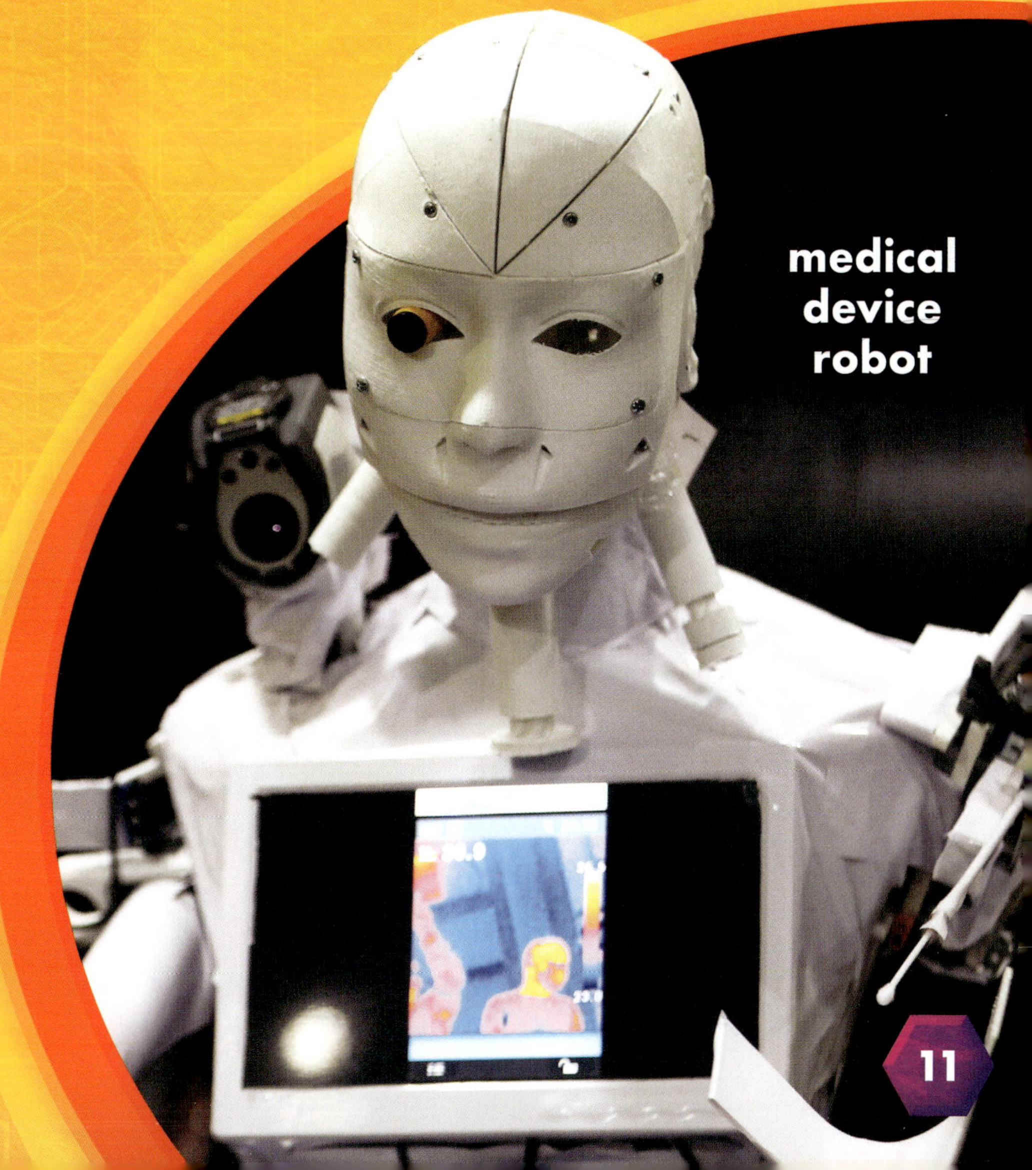

medical device robot

Many work to make **manufacturing** easier. They create or improve machines for **factories**. The machines move items. They put things together quickly.

Using STEM

try different shapes, parts, and building methods

use computers to make plans

design things that meet people's needs

find out how big or strong machines must be

This saves companies money. It makes workers' jobs safer and easier!

Mechanical engineers make sure machines are safe. They make sure machines are built to last.

They study how machines can affect people and the **environment**. They try to fix problems before machines are sold.

Becoming a Mechanical Engineer

Mechanical engineers go to college. They take many math and science classes. They use special computer programs. They learn to build things.

Many continue school after college. They choose a subject to study further.

They find jobs after school. They work at businesses or in the government. They become part of a team.

They learn on the job by starting with simpler tasks. They may study parts or check quality.

They gain knowledge and skills. They may lead projects or companies.

They use math and science every day. They find creative ways to solve problems. Their work improves lives!

Glossary

climate change—a human-caused change in Earth's weather due to warming temperatures

design—a plan for building a machine or other object

environment—the natural world

factories—buildings where products are made

fossil fuels—fuels such as coal, oil, and natural gas that were formed in the earth from plant or animal remains

labs—buildings or rooms with special tools to do science experiments and tests

manufacturing—turning raw materials into useful products

medical devices—tools used for medical purposes such as checking for or treating health issues

prosthetic—related to body parts that are human-made

quality—how well-made something is

sensors—devices that detect things like light or pressure

To Learn More

AT THE LIBRARY

Owings, Lisa. *Aerospace Engineer.* Minneapolis, Minn.: Bellwether Media, 2024.

Stanford, Olivia, and Radhika Haswani, eds. *First How Things Work Encyclopedia*. New York, N.Y.: DK Publishing, 2019.

Taylor, Diane C. *Engineers: with STEM Projects for Kids*. Junction, Vt.: Nomad Press, 2019.

ON THE WEB

FACTSURFER

Factsurfer.com gives you a safe, fun way to find more information.

1. Go to www.factsurfer.com.
2. Enter "mechanical engineer" into the search box and click 🔍.
3. Select your book cover to see a list of related content.

Index

The images in this book are reproduced through the courtesy of: KlingSup, front cover (mechanical engineer); Natalia Time, front cover (background), pp. 12-13; Dimitris Leonidas, p. 3; yurakrasil, p. 4 (prosthetic hand); gorodenkoff, pp. 4-5, 16-17; anon_tae, pp. 6-7; zlikovec, p. 7 (medical devices); NamLong Nguyen, p. 7 (factories); glebiy, p. 7 (cars); DFree, p. 8 (Bill Nye); Hero Images Inc./ Alamy, pp. 8-9, 20-21; BulentBARIS, pp. 10-11; REUTERS/ Alamy, p. 11 (medical device robot); Cultura Creative RF/ Alamy, pp. 14-15; Suwin Puengsamrong, p. 15; chabybucko/ Getty Images, p. 16; Kim Shiflett/ NASA, pp. 18-19; rawpixels stock, p. 19; chadchai krisadapong, p. 20 (mechanical engineer); Willyam Bradberry, p. 23.